# SCHUBERT

# Mass in G

for soprano, tenor & bass soli, SATB, strings & organ,
with optional wind & timpani

*Piano reduction by Berthold Tours*

**vocal score**

Order No: NOV 07 0258

New edition, 1977. Restoration of Schubert's
original wording for the four inner movements
renders the previous vocal score unsuitable for
performance in conjunction with the new.


## ORCHESTRATION


2 Oboes or Clarinets in C (*optional*)

2 Bassoons (*optional*)

2 Trumpets in D (*optional*)

Timpani (2) (*optional*)

Strings

Organ


Full score and parts to correspond with
this vocal score are available on hire.

# Kyrie eleison

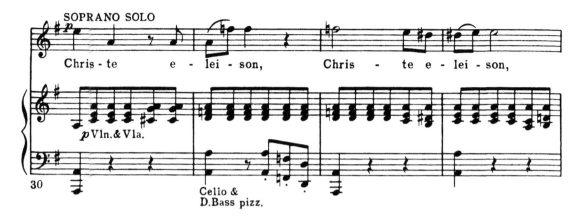

**SOPRANO SOLO**

Chris - te    e - lei - son,    Chris - te e - lei - son,

*p* Vln. & Vla.

30

Cello &
D.Bass pizz.

Chris - te    e - lei - son,    Chris - te e - lei - son,____

*fzp*

34

____    Chris-te    e - lei - son,    Chris - te e-

*p*

38

*cresc.*    *f*

lei - son,    Chris - te    e - lei - - - -

*cresc.*    *fp*

42

# Gloria in excelsis

De - us Pa - ter, om - ni - - po -

De - us Pa - ter, om - ni - - po -

De - us Pa - ter, om - ni - - po -

De - us Pa - ter, om - ni - - po -

32

tens. Do - mi - ne Fi - li u - ni - ge - ni-te Je - su

tens. Do - mi - ne Fi - li u - ni - ge - ni-te Je - su

tens. Do - mi - ne Fi - li u - ni - ge - ni-te Je - su

tens. Do - mi - ne Fi - li u - ni - ge - ni-te Je - su

35

18

# Credo

Spi - ri - tu Sanc - to, ex Ma - ri - a Vir - gi - ne; et

Spi - ri - tu Sanc - to, ex Ma - ri - a Vir - gi - ne; et

Spi - ri - tu Sanc - to, ex Ma - ri - a Vir - gi - ne; et

Spi - ri - tu Sanc - to, ex Ma - ri - a Vir - gi - ne; et

ho - mo fac - tus est.

ho - mo fac - tus est.

ho - mo fac - tus est.

ho - mo fac - tus est.

cresc.

pas - sus, et se - pul - tus est.

pas - sus, et se - pul - tus est.

pas - sus, et se - pul - tus est.

pas - sus, et se - pul - tus est.

*legato*

85

91

34

glo - ri - a, ju - di - ca - re vi -

glo - ri - a, ju - di - ca - re vi -

glo - ri - a, ju - di - ca - re vi -

glo - ri - a, ju - di - ca - re vi -

117

vos et mor - tu - os; cu - jus

vos et mor - tu - os; cu - jus

vos et mor - tu - os; cu - jus

vos et mor - tu - os; cu - jus

122

# Sanctus

42

20203

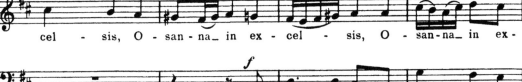

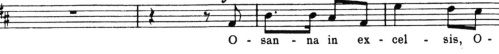

san - na in ex - cel - sis, O - san - na in ex-

san - na in ex - cel - sis, O - san - na in ex-

san - na in ex - cel - sis, O - san - na in ex-

san - na in ex - cel - sis, O - san - na in ex-

31

cel - sis.

cel - sis.

cel - sis.

cel - sis.

34

# Benedictus

ve - nit, be - ne - dic - tus,

Do - mi - ni, be - ne - dic - tus,

27

be - ne - dic - tus, be - ne - dic - tus_ in_

be - ne - dic - tus qui ve - nit_ in_

29

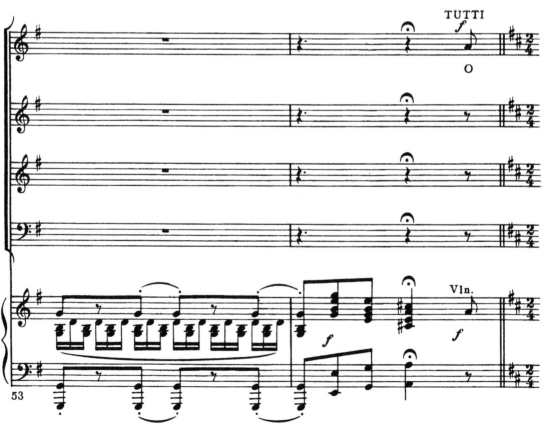

san - na in ex - cel - sis. O -

TUTTI f

O - san-na in ex - cel - sis, O - san-na in ex -

cel - sis, O - san - na, O - san-na in ex - cel - sis, O -

san - na in ex - cel - sis, O - san-na in ex - cel - sis, O -

63

san - na, O - san-na in ex - cel - sis, O -

cel - sis, O - san - na in ex-cel - sis, O -

san - na, O - san-na in ex - cel - sis, O -

san - na in ex - cel - sis, in ex-cel - sis,

67

san - na in ex - cel - sis, O - san - na in ex -
san - na in ex - cel - sis, O - san - na in ex -
san - na in ex - cel - sis, O - san - na in ex -
O - san - na in ex -

71

cel - sis, O - san - na, O - san - na in ex -
cel - sis, O - san - na, O - san - na in ex -
cel - sis, O - san - na, O - san - na in ex -
cel - sis, O - san - na, O - san - na in ex -

74

cel - sis, O - san - na in ex - cel - -

cel - sis, O - san - na in ex - cel - -

cel - sis, O - san - na in ex - cel - -

cel - sis, O - san - na in ex - cel - -

77

sis.

sis.

sis.

sis.

80

# Agnus Dei

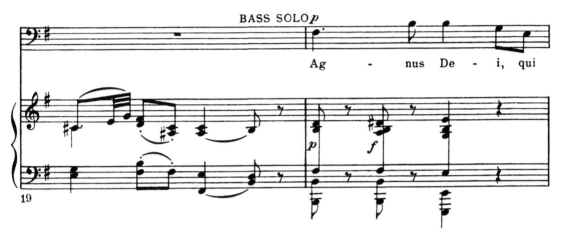